IMAGES
of America

SOUTH BEND

INDIANA

L.E. Kronewitter was of German decent and migrated from Pennsylvania to farm in South Bend. His descendants still live in the area. This photo was taken about 1900. (Maureen Kronewitter Thomson)

IMAGES
of America

SOUTH BEND

INDIANA

Kay Marnon Danielson

ARCADIA
PUBLISHING

Published by Arcadia Publishing
Charleston, South Carolina

Library of Congress Catalog Card Number: 2001089400

For all general information contact Arcadia Publishing at:
Telephone 843-853-2070
Fax 843-853-0044
E-mail sales@arcadiapublishing.com
For customer service and orders:
Toll-Free 1-888-313-2665

Visit us on the Internet at www.arcadiapublishing.com

In 1945, this photograph was taken of two boys growing up at Hudson Lake, New Carlisle. (Dennis Danielson.)

CONTENTS

ACKNOWLEDGMENTS

Undertaking a project 750 miles from where I live required a lot of help from family, friends, and new contacts in Indiana. My thanks and appreciation belongs to all of them, and especially to Harriet Witwer Marnon who always believes in what I do.

This book would not have been possible without the generosity of the local public and private institutions that gave access to their files and photographs. They included the following: St. Joseph County Public Library, Mishawaka–Penn Public Library, Hannah Lindahl Children's Museum, Studebaker National Museum Archives, The Archives of The University of Notre Dame, Saint Mary's College Archives, Purdue University Cooperative Extension Service, Honeywell, Northern Indiana Historical Society Inc., and the *South Bend Tribune*, as well as numerous individuals that came forth with precious photographs from the past.

There are many fine histories written on specific areas of local interest that were most helpful in collecting information for this book. Some I found most useful included: *The University of Notre Dame, A Portrait of Its History and Campus* by Schlereth, *Legends and Losers* by Andy Jones, *A Mishawaka Mosaic* by David Eisen, *Our City, South Bend, Indiana* by Ball and Davis, *A Pictorial History of Indiana* by Hoover.

My gratitude goes to all those people, professional and amateur, who stood behind the lens and recorded their vision on film.

INTRODUCTION

Before recorded history, the Indians knew the bounty of the northern Indiana area and most importantly, the portage that gave them water access to lands from the Great Lakes to the Gulf of Mexico. When the fur traders established business with the Indians, the missionaries followed. Then European-born men and their descendants were making claim to the land.

While the northern two-thirds of the territory was still wilderness, Indiana became a state on December 11, 1816. When Pierre Navarre cut logs and built a cabin on the banks of the St. Joseph River, it opened the northern Indiana area for further settlement. Iron bogs near Mishawaka drew men of commerce as early as 1830 to dig the ore and shape the course of the community. The St. Joseph River served both villages, providing power and transportation to encourage new ventures. Flat, rich soils, and a climate that provided warmth and moisture to produce fine crops, drew men of the land to feed the small towns that began to grow.

The people came speaking many languages. Polish, Hungarian, Swedish, German, Irish, English, Belgian, and African-American dialects were heard, and each brought their ways of worship. While Catholic priests were the first to settle, Methodist, Episcopalian, Christian, Presbyterian, and others soon set their roots.

This book attempts to tell one version of that history, and the story is shaped by the images that were available to the author. It is by no means comprehensive, but reflects the flavor of the times. The book offers a look at the variety of commerce, schools, people, activities, and residences. It is visual piece of the history of St. Joseph County, South Bend, and Mishawaka.

Some things have not changed since 1942—children still like to ride in little red wagons. (Harriet Witwer Marnon.)

Some photographic studios dressed up the back of their portrait cards with fanciful designs as well as fantastic claims. The backs could be as entertaining and informative as the photographs on the front, taken in 1890. (Maureen Kronewitter Thomson.)

One

COMMERCE, INDUSTRY, AND AGRICULTURE

In the mid-1800s, the country was expanding westward, and the Studebaker Manufacturing Company was producing wagon transport for the pioneers. This Conestoga wagon ferried families over the prairie to their new homes and now resides in the Studebaker National Museum. (From the collection of Studebaker National Museum, South Bend, Indiana.)

Henry and Clem started their blacksmith shop in 1852 at the corner of Michigan and Jefferson Streets in South Bend, and the company eventually grew to include brothers J.M., Peter, and Jacob Studebaker. (From the collection of St. Joseph County Public Library.)

The Studebaker Wagon Works grew to be the largest wagon manufacturer in the world, and the only business of its kind to successfully switch from horse drawn conveyances to gasoline powered vehicles. The company produced an electric car in 1902, and a gas-propelled model in 1904. (From the collection of Dennis Danielson.)

In the early part of the century, many women worked in the factories and they certainly did most of the clerical work in this office. (From the collection of Studebaker National Museum, South Bend, Indiana.)

In 1926, this young woman tied and covered springs for the Studebaker automobile seats. (From the collection of Studebaker National Museum, South Bend, Indiana.)

Giant sheet-metal presses stamp and shape automobile bodies. (From the collection of Studebaker National Museum, South Bend, Indiana.)

The 1947 assembly lines were geared for personal cars and produced the Champions after fulfilling government military contracts during World War II. (From the collection of Studebaker National Museum, South Bend, Indiana.)

Hoods pressed and stacked were on their way to the assembly line. One man remembers welding two of these hoods together to make a boat. (From the collection of Studebaker National Museum, South Bend, Indiana.)

Used for testing cold weather conditions, cars were often frozen like the one shown in 1936. However, the "Ice Car" was also used as a publicity stunt. A new 1934 Studebaker Dictator was incased with ice a foot thick and weighing 4,000 pounds. A young woman, who volunteered to enter the car from under the floorboards, was "discovered" inside after four hours when police rescue squads had chipped away enough ice for her to get out. (From the collection of Studebaker National Museum, South Bend, Indiana.)

Established in 1926, the 800-acre Studebaker Proving Grounds (now Bendix Woods County Park) was used to test automobiles. In 1938, 8,259 white pine trees were planted and eventually grew to what the Guinness Book of World Records calls the largest living sign with each letter over 200-feet wide, 200-feet long, and 60-feet tall. (From the collection of Studebaker National Museum, South Bend, Indiana.)

Known as the largest car in the world, the model of a 1931 President 8 Convertible stood at the entrance of the Studebaker Proving Grounds until being scraped for metal during World War II. (From the collection of Studebaker National Museum, South Bend, Indiana.)

This 1935 Studebaker Commander appeared in the movie *The Color Purple*. (From the collection of Studebaker National Museum, South Bend, Indiana.)

Hollywood stars were often used in Studebaker advertisements. In this instance, Mickey Rooney stands proudly by the 1935 Commander Land Cruiser. (From the collection of Studebaker National Museum, South Bend, Indiana.)

Here, Harpo Marx is shown with a Champion Coupe in 1947. (From the collection of Studebaker National Museum, South Bend, Indiana.)

At the turn of the century, when gasoline powered automobiles made an appearance, gasoline filling and service stations followed. Some were distinctive architecture, and regrettably, few—like the Consumers #18 in Mishawaka—remain. (From the collection of Mishawaka-Penn Public Library.)

It seems impossible, but in the 1920s gas was once just 12¢ a gallon in Mishawaka. (From the collection of Mishawaka-Penn Public Library.)

A few of these charming little buildings remain around the country, but this Conoco gas and service station in Mishawaka is long gone. (From the collection of Mishawaka-Penn Public Library.)

You could get lubrication, motor and brake work, as well as a car wash at Knoblock's Auto Service and Auto Laundry in Mishawaka. It was torn down in the 1970s. (From the collection of Mishawaka-Penn Public Library.)

As long as there have been automobiles, there has been a need for wrecker services. This photograph was taken in the early-1900s. (From the collection of Mishawaka-Penn Public Library.)

The automobile also changed the face of America as roads were built to accommodate the increased traffic. This road paving crew helped with that task. (From the collection of Mishawaka-Penn Public Library.)

Scottish immigrant James Oliver came to the United States in 1837, eventually creating the Oliver Chilled Plow Works complex at 701 South Chapin. He bought interest in a South Bend foundry that made cast iron plows, bedsteads, pulleys, window weights, Singer sewing machine bases, and Studebaker wagon runners in 1855. Oliver secured 45 patents on his plow designs, overshadowing all his other products. (From the collection of Historic Preservation Commission of South Bend & St. Joseph County.)

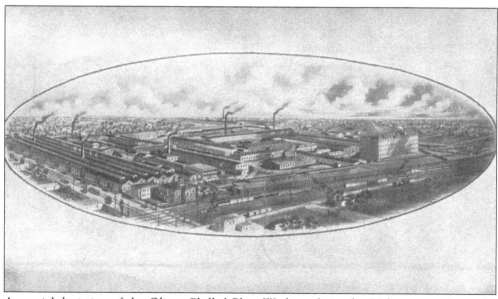

An aerial depiction of the Oliver Chilled Plow Works early in the 20th century shows the extensive factory physical plant. (From the collection of St. Joseph County Public Library.)

This group of young women worked at the Oliver Chilled Plow Works. They represent the many women who began working in factories during World War I, 1918. (From the collection of Studebaker National Museum, South Bend, Indiana.)

Popularly known as Mishawaka's Ball Band Plant, the company had its beginnings when Jacob and his son Martin Beiger bought a small business on the St. Joseph River. Six years later in 1874, the company incorporated as the Mishawaka Woolen Manufacturing Company. They first made flannel underwear and then the All-Knit Boot (with a black band and a red ball around the top) for use with rubber overshoes. In later years the company made car mats and airplane fuel cells, eventually being purchased by Uniroyal. (From the collection of Mishawaka-Penn Public Library.)

As the Ball Band grew, the facilities frequently expanded. Factory jobs paid well for the times, and the Ball Band was the largest employer in Mishawaka for many years. (From the collection of Mishawaka-Penn Public Library.)

Patriotism ran high at the Ball Band in 1898 with banners proclaiming, "Remember the Maine." (From the collection of Mishawaka-Penn Public Library.)

The Ball Band shoe-making room was a beehive of activity, much too fast for the low light levels and slow camera shutter speeds early in the century. (From the collection of Mishawaka-Penn Public Library.)

The Ball Band employed men, women, and children in its early history. (From the collection of Mishawaka-Penn Public Library.)

Ball Band salesmen took to their horse and carriage vending their products around the county. This photograph was taken in 1905. (From the collection of Mishawaka-Penn Public Library.)

Some of the Ball Band footwear products are displayed in a department store window. (From the collection of Mishawaka-Penn Public Library.)

Many groups of employees were photographed. This was the West Shoe Room in 1936. (From the collection of Mishawaka-Penn Public Library.)

The Ball Band/Uniroyal Company contributed to Mishawaka's prosperity for over 100 years. The Ball Band was closed in 1996, and the 46-acre complex was razed for a river walk and footbridge, housing, offices, shops, and eateries in 2000. (From the collection of Mishawaka-Penn Public Library.)

Established in 1924, The Bendix Engineering Works revolutionized the use of the four-wheel brake system, and landed Vincent Bendix in South Bend when he bought facilities for his automobile brake operation that eventually went into airplane brakes and struts. This photograph was taken in 1930. (From the collection of Honeywell Corporation.)

The 1934 Bendix SWC (Steel Wheel Corporation.) was a one of a kind. Developed in secrecy to showcase new products for automobiles, it was completed in 1934 after 2.5 years of work at a cost of $84,000. The gray sedan had a six-cylinder Continental engine with fastback styling, front-wheel drive, four-wheel independent suspension, a fan-less cooling system, electric vacuum gearshift, slotted wheel covers to air cool the breaks, dual windshield wipers, jumbo tires, some aluminum body panels, and a clock in the hub of the steering wheel. The Bendix Car is now in the Studebaker National Museum in South Bend. (From the collection of Honeywell Corporation.)

Vincent Bendix (right) awards the first Air Trophy to Jimmy Doolittle in 1931 for flying his Solution at an average speed of 223 MPH from Los Angeles to Cleveland in 9 hours and 10 minutes. (From the collection of Honeywell Corporation.)

Amelia Earhart participated in the Bendix Transcontinental Air Races, and this photo may be from a brief visit to South Bend when she landed at Bendix Airport in 1937. Other well-known pilots like Roscoe Turner, Jacqueline Cochran, and Howard Hughes vied for the coveted Air Trophy. Captain John T. Walton won the last race in 1962, flying coast to coast in 2 hours and 1 minute with his B-58. (From the collection of Honeywell Corporation.)

Here we see the Bendix assembly line in the 1950s. It all began when 16-year-old Vincent Bendix ran away from his Moline, Illinois home in 1898. He worked various jobs including motorcycle manufacturing, where he learned about internal combustion engines and powered vehicles. In 1907, he formed an automobile company—the same year 94 new automobile makes were introduced. While his automobile firm didn't last, he was convinced the automobile industry had to have a mechanical starter to avoid the hazards (broken arms) and inconvenience of hand cranking. He successfully developed the Bendix Starter Drive and was on his way in the new automotive industry and later, in aviation. (From the collection of Honeywell Corporation.)

Bendix airplane brakes and struts required cold-weather testing. The company also produced pressure carburetors used in virtually every aircraft in the Allied arsenal in World War II, and even produced home appliances including the Bendix washing machine. (From the collection of Honeywell Corporation.)

Created by Bendix during World War II, the pilot Capt. Ben Dix comic strip illustrated the "Invisible Crew" that helped him through his adventures. The strip, aimed at industry suppliers, included diagrams of the Stromberg injection carburetor, Eclipse aircraft starter, the Gibson Girl radio transmitter, and other instruments the company produced. (From the collection of Honeywell Corporation.)

Employees from the South Bend Lathe Works go through a scrap pile. (From the collection of Studebaker National Museum, South Bend, Indiana.)

The South Bend Lathe Works produced motor driven lathes, some of which were used to make munitions. At one point the company went into Chapter 11, and was purchased by the employees. (From the collection of Studebaker National Museum, South Bend, Indiana.)

First established in 1868, the Singer Manufacturing Company's Cabinet Factory in South Bend made cabinets, iron stands, and treadle and wheel for sewing machines. Drawn to the area for the rich resources of native oak and walnut as well as bog iron, 600 varieties of Singers were shipped around the world. (From the collection of Studebaker National Museum, South Bend, Indiana.)

After a long day of work, these men and boys leave work at the Singer plant in 1908. Moved from a river location to Western Avenue in 1900, the 76-acre complex included a foundry, drying kilns, cabinetry buildings, and incinerators. (From the collection of Studebaker National Museum, South Bend, Indiana.)

These boys worked at Singer as part of the workforce that included many youth in the early-1900s. (From the collection of Studebaker National Museum, South Bend, Indiana.)

Getting your company name before a crowd was good advertisement. This entry prepares for the 1923 parade. The company also sponsored many sports activities, and the Singer baseball team won the city factory league competition three-years running. (From the collection of Studebaker National Museum, South Bend, Indiana.)

The South Bend Singer operation made cabinets for the sewing machines, and these men are sanding cases on power equipment. The company closed in 1954 due to a depleted source of hardwoods. (From the collection of Studebaker National Museum, South Bend, Indiana.)

The Singer sewing machine was used in industry as well as by individuals at home. (From the collection of Mishawaka-Penn Public Library.)

34

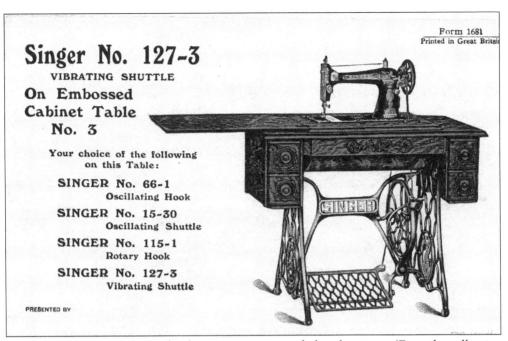

The Singer Company often utilized inexpensive postcards for advertising. (From the collection of Studebaker National Museum, South Bend, Indiana.)

This charming postcard illustrates one of the more unusual uses for the Singer sewing machine. It also advises that "You can try one Free" and old machines are taken in exchange. (From the collection of Studebaker National Museum, South Bend, Indiana.)

South Bend Watch Company.

The South Bend Watch Company operated from 1903 to 1929 on Mishawaka Avenue. At one time it employed 600, and annually produced 60,000 of the "Watch With a Purple Ribbon." Today the pocket watches are a prized collectable. (From the collection of Studebaker National Museum, South Bend, Indiana.)

These young businessmen had to learn the ropes, and that often took them into the factory. (From the collection of Hannah Lindahl Children's Museum.)

In 1878, the original Dodge Manufacturing at 500 South Union was an important addition to Mishawaka's economy. At first making wood specialties, the company changed with the times and ownership to produce industrial rope pulleys, split-friction clutches, mounted anti-friction bearings, and contributed marine bearings and stern tubes to the World War II effort. Eventually bought out by Reliance Electric of Cleveland and Exxon Corporation, most operations were moved out, effectively closing Dodge in 1982. (From the collection of Hannah Lindahl Children's Museum.)

A Dodge Manufacturing truck was a familiar sight on the streets of Mishawaka in 1911. (From the collection of Mishawaka-Penn Public Library.)

Seen here are the Merchant Flouring Mills, City Roller Mills, and Phoenix Mills at 111 East Market Street, South Bend. They were manufacturers of Our Pride, Bon Ton, Jack Frost, Buckwheat, and Rye Flours. Feed ground to order, *c.* 1889. (From the collection of Dennis Danielson.)

In the days before everyone could afford an automobile, this Mishawaka livery stable was the place to rent a conveyance. (From the collection of Hannah Lindahl Children's Museum.)

Seen here in 1889 are South Bend National Bank, located at 129 North Michigan Street, and D.B.J. Schafer Staple and Fancy Groceries, at 131 North Michigan Street, South Bend. (From the collection of Dennis Danielson.)

The late-1800s architecture included fancy adornment on and in houses. Meyer & Poehlman were pleased to supply galvanized cornice works, hardware, stoves, and tin ware. (From the collection of Dennis Danielson.)

Express has taken on new meaning in our modern life. In 1889, the word meant horse and wagon transportation with the U.S. Express Co. (From the collection of Dennis Danielson.)

Made in South Bend, the Birdsell alfalfa and clover hullers were horse drawn machines that gave farmers the opportunity to market clover seeds. Long before chemical fertilizers, the nitrogen-rich clover crop was used in crop rotation to enrich the soil. Farmers with hullers could produce seed for their own use as well as for sale. (From the collection of Studebaker National Museum, South Bend, Indiana.)

OPINIONS OF OTHERS
What you should know about
· THE BIRDSELL ·
ALFALFA HULLERS

SOUTH BEND, IND., U.S.A.

B. Kempner & Bro. clothing retail store was located on the corner of Washington and Main Streets in South Bend, 1889. While the manikins on the sidewalk had no problem standing still for the long exposure required for the photograph, some of the pedestrians blurred while walking through the picture. (From the collection of Dennis Danielson.)

Pictured here is L. Nickel Jr., & Co., popular caterers, wholesale and retail grocers, and Vienna Bakery Restaurant and Grocery. It was located at 119 to 123 North Main, South Bend, in 1889. And, you could have your books bound next door. (From the collection of Dennis Danielson.)

In 1889, A. McDonald, artistic photographer who started business in 1861, was located in a quiet neighborhood at the corner of Michigan and Wayne Streets, South Bend. The photographer advertised portraits and crayon work in his window, and was reported to be the first ground level studio in Indiana. Most studios were situated on top floors of buildings, using available skylights. The business is still in operation. (From the collection of Dennis Danielson.)

In 1889, a trip to the dentist could not have been a pleasure. Still, D.E. Cummins, D.D.S. did his best, welcoming patients to his Dental Palace at Main and Market Streets, South Bend. (From the collection of Dennis Danielson.)

In January 1900, these men served the Lake Shore & Michigan Southern Railroad as the Freight Office Staff warmed by the wood-burning stove in the center of the room. The line is now the New York Central, Mishawaka. (From the collection of Hannah Lindahl Children's Museum.)

The Distler Plumbing & Heating Co. employees pose for a photograph in Mishawaka, c. 1910. (From the collection of Mishawaka-Penn Public Library.)

George Wyman & Company began merchandising dry goods, carpets, etc. in 1860 on Michigan Street, South Bend. As the operation grew and expanded, the business moved into its own building and served the community as one of the leading department stores until closing in 1972 and demolished in 1973. (From the collection of Dennis Danielson.)

With the automobile came some amazing claims to performance, like the 100,000 miles locked in low gear from Speed Mike Auto Sales, Mishawaka, in 1938. (From the collection of Mishawaka-Penn Public Library.)

The Jordan Brothers Transfer truck is empty and ready to move your goods. This photograph was taken in 1919 in Mishawaka. (From the collection of Mishawaka-Penn Public Library.)

The Trulley Funeral Service limousine was sleek and luxurious for that last ride. This photograph was taken in the 1930s in Mishawaka. (From the collection of Mishawaka-Penn Public Library.)

North Main Street was a vital business district in the 1920s. Even then trash-cans urged, "Help Keep Mishawaka Clean." (From the collection of Mishawaka-Penn Public Library.)

SOUTH BEND TOY MANUFACTURING COMPANY • SOUTH BEND, INDIANA

The South Bend Toy Manufacturing Company catalog from 1941-42 shows a few of the extensive toy items. Although most of the products were made for children, the South Bend Toy croquet sets were produced for the adult market and professional competitions. (From the collection of Studebaker National Museum, South Bend, Indiana.)

Streetcars provided convenient and economical transportation around Mishawaka and South Bend in 1890. (From the collection of Hanna Lindahl Children's Museum.)

Beginning in 1903, the South Shore trains ran from Chicago to South Bend, stopping at the South Shore train station that stood at Michigan and LaSalle Streets. A tunnel under the street connected the station with the LaSalle Hotel, protecting visitors from inclement weather. The train station was torn down in 1974. The only interurban train to survive into the new century, the South Shore now stations at the South Bend Airport known as the Michiana Regional/South Bend Transportation Center. (From the collection of St. Joseph County Library.)

The family-owned Gates Chevrolet Dealership in Mishawaka has supplied and serviced automobiles to area customers since 1933. While the company is still in business and has moved, this 1956 photograph shows the long-time location on Lincoln Way East. (From the collection of Mishawaka-Penn Public Library.)

The South Bend Bait Company began operations in the early-1900s, and quickly established a loyal following all over the country with over 3,000 fly-fishing and bait-casting items including their Callmac Bass Bug, Trout-Oreno, Surf-Oreno, and the South Bend Babe-Oreno. (From the collection of Studebaker National Museum, South Bend, Indiana.)

Sidewalk sales were a frequent and enjoyable part of shopping downtown. This picture was taken in 1965 in Mishawaka. (From the collection of Mishawaka-Penn Public Library.)

This street scene in South Bend in the 1920s displays a time period in which you could see a movie at the Granada, ride the streetcar, stop in at Hooks, buy men's clothing at Richmans, or take a 25¢ cab ride. (From the collection of *South Bend Tribune*.)

Prices were pretty reasonable at the soda fountain and lunch counters of the 1950s, where you could belly up to the bar and dine on Chile con Carni, a Coca-Cola, and a banana split for 75¢. (From the collection of St. Joseph County Public Library.)

The Kewpie Doll was a familiar sight on top of the Kewpee's Restaurant at 327 North Michigan, South Bend, in the 30s, 40s, and 50s. One of the first franchises in the country, Kewpee was founded in the 1920s in Racine, Wisconsin, and featured hand-patted hamburgers and frosted malteds. (From the collection of St. Joseph County Public Library.)

First delivering milk in horse-drawn wagons, the Mishawaka Dairy served the community for many years. (From the collection of Hannah Lindahl Children's Museum.)

When milk production went from the farm to the commercial dairy, there was stiff competition. This is the Farmer's Dairy in Mishawaka. (From the collection of Hannah Lindahl Children's Museum.)

Agriculture was a vital part of early settlement commerce and it remains important today. Members of the Studebaker family owned the South Bend Hereford and Jersey Cattle Co. in 1889. (From the collection of Dennis Danielson.)

Built in 1920, the Mishawaka Grain and Coal Company on South Union was a regular stop for farmers and urban dwellers alike until the 1950s. (From the collection of Mishawaka-Penn Public Library.)

The farmer's market was a familiar scene in both large and small communities in St. Joseph County in 1915. (From the collection of Purdue University Cooperative Extension Service.)

Fantastic barns were part of the landscape when animals, forage, and farm implements had to be stored away from a harsh winter climate. Unfortunately, few like this dairy barn remain today. (From the collection of Purdue University Cooperative Extension Service.)

Even though they had the use of early tractors, harvesting the hay was a laborious job that still required many hands. This photograph was taken in 1916. (From the collection of Purdue University Cooperative Extension Service.)

Feeding the hogs also drew attention from the farm cats and chickens. (From the collection of Purdue University Cooperative Extension Service.)

Then as now, farm field days provided farmers with the latest information from the local extension service, a chance to visit with their peers, and usually a great lunch. This photograph was taken in the 1920s. (From the collection of Purdue University Cooperative Extension Service.)

Preparing the soil was a difficult work for any man, but sometimes women or children had to take the reins to get the job done. (From the collection of Purdue University Cooperative Extension Service.)

Educating youth as well as adults has always been an important part of the Extension Service efforts. These children are learning about dairy practices in 1916. (From the collection of Purdue University Cooperative Extension Service.)

This mechanized version of planting potatoes saved the farmer a lot of time and labor. (From the collection of Purdue University Cooperative Extension Service.)

At one time, celery was a viable crop in St. Joseph County. (From the collection of Purdue University Cooperative Extension Service.)

After some produce was harvested, it was given a hot water treatment before being shipped to market. (From the collection of Purdue University Cooperative Extension Service.)

At the end of a long growing season, farmers celebrated the fruits of their labors with county fairs and competitions of all kinds. This group tested their skills at poultry calling in 1921. (From the collection of Purdue University Cooperative Extension Service.)

Fall was the season for the annual Fruit Festival, an occasion for dress up clothes and sampling the goods. This photograph was taken in 1922. (From the collection of Purdue University Cooperative Extension Service.)

In 1922, this home economics club met for a picnic. (From the collection of Purdue University Cooperative Extension Service.)

This group of farm kids went to summer camp in 1926. (From the collection of Purdue University Cooperative Extension Service.)

At one time, many people relied heavily on strong horses for much of the strenuous agricultural work. Notre Dame bred draft animals for their own agricultural studies and to raise produce for the college. The breeding program was also used to strengthen local stock. (From the collection of Purdue University Cooperative Extension Service.)

This man was justifiably proud of his crop of rye. (From the collection of Purdue University Cooperative Extension Service.)

Two

EDUCATION

A wooden meeting place built by Father Claude Allouez in 1686 was first on the spot that was to become Notre Dame, but later abandoned. Father Badin, the first priest ordained in the United States built a chapel in there in 1830. Shown here, the Log Cabin Chapel, rebuilt in 1906 on the site of the original cabin that burned in 1858, remains on the grounds of present Notre Dame as a reminder of the great institution's beginnings. The chapel is still in use for religious services. (From the collection of The Archives of The University of Notre Dame.)

In 1842 at the age of 28, French-born Father Theodore Frederick Sorin came to organize Notre Dame University with 10 acres of land and a budget of $400. He became the school's first president, and within two years he had a brick building where students were educated. The Legislature of Indiana chartered Notre Dame on January 15, 1844, to grant degrees of liberal arts, sciences, law, and medicine. Sorin retired in 1865, and died in 1893. (From the collection of The Archives of The University of Notre Dame.)

The 1899 Notre Dame Volunteer Fire Crew was a vital part of the university, as fire was an all too frequent hazard. In 1879, the main building was totally destroyed by fire. (From the collection of The Archives of The University of Notre Dame.)

Holy Cross Sisters came to Notre Dame from France in 1843. They staffed laundries, infirmaries, kitchens, set type in the University Press, bound books, were tailors, gardeners, seamstresses, char women, and staffed the St. Edwards' Minims School for 6,000 elementary-school-aged boys at Notre Dame. These sisters take a break from their cooking duties to enjoy some music and dance. (From the collection of The Archives of The University of Notre Dame.)

Here we see Professor Hoynes with his Notre Dame law school class in Sorin Hall around 1900. (From the collection of The Archives of The University of Notre Dame.)

The well-equipped school library was vital to the university then as now. The current library has a collection of nearly 3-million books. (From the collection of The Archives of The University of Notre Dame.)

Thanks to people like these Notre Dame photographers, the school's rich history is well documented from the earliest days of images on film. (From the collection of The Archives of The University of Notre Dame.)

Students were forbidden to own vehicles, but a streetcar line carried them to the city for recreation and to hook up with transportation home for vacations. This photograph was taken in 1916. During football games, 15 or 20 trains would line up to carry spectators home. By 1940, the streetcars were gone. (From the collection of The Archives of The University of Notre Dame.)

The path between Notre Dame and Saint Mary's College was well trod in all kinds of weather. (From the collection of The Archives of The University of Notre Dame.)

The Notre Dame sports tradition began with a game against Michigan University in 1887. By 1894, Notre Dame grandstand ticket sales were still fairly economical and there was no standing in line. (From the collection of The Archives of The University of Notre Dame.)

Knute Rockne entered Notre Dame in 1910 in the science school, and participated in running and pole vaulting as well as theater productions and editing the school magazine. He graduated *magna cum laud* in chemistry and joined the Notre Dame staff. In 1918, he became athletic director and head coach. In the next 13 years, Rockne created an extraordinary football legend. (From the collection of The Archives of The University of Notre Dame.)

Knute Rockne is seen on the right directing football practice in the stadium that was to become known as the home of the Fighting Irish. On this day in 1925, Babe Ruth, who was in town for a Yankee exhibition baseball game, stopped in to throw a few passes. (From the collection of The Archives of The University of Notre Dame.)

Knute Rockne's untimely death came in 1931 at the age of 43 in a Kansas airplane crash. His funeral was held on campus in Sacred Heart Church and was attended by notables from around the country. (From the collection of The Archives of The University of Notre Dame.)

Three companies of military units were part of campus life in 1890, but the units were not directly associated with a national military service. (From the collection of The Archives of The University of Notre Dame.)

Cycling was a popular activity, and for some it was the only means of transportation other than walking. (From the collection of The Archives of The University of Notre Dame.)

Today, the early-1900s equipment looks primitive but it was considered very good at the time. (From the collection of The Archives of The University of Notre Dame.)

A building boom in the 1960s dramatically changed the look of the campus. (From the collection of The Archives of The University of Notre Dame.)

St. Mary's College was originally established by the Holy Cross sisters in 1843 in Bertrand, Michigan, and moved to South Bend in 1855. These photographs of various buildings were taken in1889. (From the collection of Dennis Danielson.)

The first legally authorized Catholic women's college in the United States, St. Mary's established an active alumni group. These women were pictured in 1901. (From the collection of Saint Mary's College Archives.)

This construction on LeMans in 1925 was just part of the on-going expansion of the college. (From the collection of Saint Mary's College Archives.)

This small Hummer School at Madison and Mulberry Roads in Mishawaka offered schooling to rural children. This photograph was taken in 1900. (From the collection of Hannah Lindahl Children's Museum.).

Located beside the two lane, U.S. Highway 31 North in Roseland, this Ullery School first-grade class had their group picture taken in 1948. (From the collection of Harriet Witwer Marnon.)

Twin Branch School taught children of all ages. This photograph was taken in 1880. (From the collection of Hannah Lindahl Children's Museum.)

The Osceola School is pictured about 1908. (From the collection of Hannah Lindahl Children's Museum.)

The Mishawaka High School Band was outfitted and ready to play in 1934. (From the collection of Mishawaka-Penn Public Library.)

Three

PUBLIC BUILDINGS, PLACES, AND SERVANTS

Built in 1872, the South Bend Post Office and Federal Library served the city for many years before being replaced by new facilities. (From the collection of St. Joseph County Public Library.)

The First Presbyterian Trinitarian Society of the Village of St. Joseph Iron Works was established in Mishawaka in 1834. Built in 1888, the South Bend Presbyterian Church, seen here at 101 South Lafayette, still stands today, but its future is uncertain. (From the collection of Historic Preservation Commission of South Bend & St. Joseph County.)

Ready for guests in December 1899, the Oliver Hotel hosted over 2,000 for the gala grand opening. Built by James Oliver, it was lauded as the best and most magnificent hotel in Indiana and one of the finest in the United States. The Oliver had 136 rooms that rented for $2 to $4 a day. (From the collection of St. Joseph County Public Library.)

Built by James Oliver in 1885, the lavishly decorated Oliver Opera House provided a place for theater entertainment at costs ranging from 25¢ for gallery seats to $1 for orchestra chairs. (From the collection of Dennis Danielson.)

Established in 1861, the Turner's organization was German in origin and encouraged physical exercise.(From the collection of Dennis Danielson.)

This photograph of a Salvation Army Flood Relief truck was taken in 1930. (From the collection of Mishawaka-Penn Public Library.)

The Mishawaka Orphans' Home was family and shelter for hundreds of children. It was built in 1907, and burned in 1979. This photograph was taken in the 1940s. (From the collection of Mishawaka-Penn Public Library.)

Here we see the Mishawaka Orphans' Home dining hall. (From the collection of Mishawaka-Penn Public Library.)

The Mishawaka/South Bend Street Car Line shown here on the Main Street Bridge in 1910 Mishawaka, provided transportation between the two cities and had side tracks to many factories. Horses and mules pulled the trains for three years until they were replaced with electric power in 1888. A train ride to South Bend took 45 minutes by mule and 15 minutes with electric. Tickets were 10¢. (From the collection of Hannah Lindahl Children's Museum.)

The Hen Island Dam is one of two dams on the St. Joseph River in Mishawaka. It was constructed in 1902. (From the collection of Hannah Lindahl Children's Museum.)

This is a bird's-eye view of South Bend from a 225-foot tower looking west was taken in 1889. (From the collection of Dennis Danielson.)

Northern Indiana winters mean snow, sometimes a lot of snow. This 1906 storm left the intersection of Lincolnway West at Church Street in Mishawaka closed to all traffic except foot and trolley. (From the collection of Hannah Lindahl Children's Museum.)

Built in 1833, the original building was known as Hurd's Tavern, and later Milbourn House. After fire destroyed the previous, the Mishawaka Hotel served the community on the site for many years, and then was cleared for the current post office in 1970. (From the collection of Mishawaka-Penn Public Library.)

Mishawaka's firemen posed for this picture at the Main St. Station in the 1930s. (From the collection of Hannah Lindahl Children's Museum.)

One of South Bend's finest, this police officer served his community around 1900. (From the collection of Don Cornelis.)

These South Bend police officers walked a city beat in 1890, and the mustaches seem as much a part of the uniform as the hats. (From the collection of Don Cornelis.)

The South Bend police department was well equipped with this emergency vehicle. (From the collection of Don Cornelis.)

The Dillinger Car was a 1934 custom-made Studebaker built for the South Bend Police. It had a powerful motor, a porthole in the windshield for a gun, and baffles protecting the radiator and tires. However, it was never used against the infamous criminal John Dillinger who robbed the New Carlisle National Bank in July of 1933 and the South Bend Merchants National Bank in June of 1934. Dillinger was killed the following month in Chicago trying to evade arrest, and the Dillinger Car was demolished in an automobile wreck a few years after it was made. (From the collection of Don Cornelis.)

Four

ENTERTAINMENT

Parades were an important activity in the years before radio and television substantially changed the forms of entertainment. Celebrating the state's 100th year, the 1916 Centennial Parade filed in front of the grandstand in South Bend. (From the collection of St. Joseph County Public Library.)

Children were the main participants in the Disease Prevention Day Parade, encouraging the use of Dutch Cleanser. This photograph was taken in the early-1900s in South Bend. (From the collection of St. Joseph County Public Library.)

The Disease Prevention Day Parade illustrated the dire consequences of pesky insects. Healthy children held signs that said "I Swat the Fly." A hanging skeleton obviously didn't. (From the collection of St. Joseph County Public Library.)

Parades provided a chance for people to socialize and for advertisers to inform. In 1909, the Mason's Transfer Line sign proclaimed, "When you're tired of moving, call Masons." (From the collection of Hannah Lindahl Children's Museum.)

A Christmas parade in 1960s South Bend is much the same as bygone days, except for the modern clothing and automobiles. (From the collection of *South Bend Tribune*.)

Professor Dancing Class is shown at their 1898 recital in Mishawaka. (From the collection of Hannah Lindahl Children's Museum.)

One wonders just how the 1934 Hugh Talbotts Walkathon Athletic Contest contestants managed to walk very far in their formal clothing. (From the collection of Mishawaka-Penn Public Library.)

The Dolly Evans Dance Studio dancers not only had some great moves, they also had great fashions in 1930s Mishawaka. (From the collection of Mishawaka-Penn Public Library.)

Work sponsored activity groups were an active part of the social life. The Dodge Cycling Club of Mishawaka was likely gathered for a Fourth of July parade in 1889. (From the collection of Mishawaka-Penn Public Library.)

Fashions were of interest to the ladies of the 1930s, with particular attention being paid to fur adornment and stylish hats. (From the collection of Mishawaka-Penn Public Library.)

A Democratic stronghold for many years, Roosevelt supporters gather in front of The Famous Store, back when a thirsty person could get a drink of water at the sidewalk fountain. This photograph was taken in the late-1930s in Mishawaka. (From the collection of Mishawaka-Penn Public Library.)

If there is a hill and snow, there is a sled. These South Bend children would spend all day on the slope until darkness drove them home wet, cold, and happy, c. 1910. (From the collection of St. Joseph County Public Library.)

During hot summer days, the waters of Leeper Park were used to good advantage. (From the collection of Maureen Kronewitter Thomson.)

In 1913, people made their own entertainment, and ice-skating was a popular winter recreation on local ponds. (From the collection of Hannah Lindahl Children's Museum.)

Directly across from what is now the Indiana University South Bend campus on the St. Joseph River, Springbrook Park first opened in 1899, when the area served as a Northern Indiana Railway Company streetcar terminal. The grounds were a gathering place for picnics and concerts as shown in this 1913 postcard. By 1917, the park had a dance hall, an amphitheater, a midway with rides, a half-mile racetrack, and a baseball diamond. (From the collection of St. Joseph County Public Library.)

Earl J. "Pete" Redden managed the Springbrook Park for a few years, and in 1927, Redden bought the park and renamed it Playland. (From the collection of Don Cornelis.)

In the late-1920s, Miss Helen Astley and her court sat viewing the third annual Tribune-Playland baby parade as the children filed by the grandstand. (From the collection of Studebaker National Museum, South Bend, Indiana.)

The Playland racetrack tested the speed of horses as well as horse power, and the fans could hear the pounding of hooves one day and the roar of engines the next. This photograph was taken in 1927. (From the collection of Don Cornelis.)

The Playland Ballroom hosted big band dances with Cab Calloway, Tommy Dorsey, Duke Ellington, and Guy Lombardo as well as alternating as a roller-skating rink. After World War II, the rise of television and air conditioning heralded the decline and demise of amusement parks. Playland closed in the late-1960s after entertaining generations of Hoosier families. (From the collection of Mishawaka-Penn Public Library.)

It is believed it was Charles A. Lindbergh who delivered this Lincoln-Standard airplane. He piloted mail planes in St. Louis and occasionally delivered airplanes. In 1936, 11 months after this photograph was taken, Lindbergh flew the *Spirit of St. Louis* to Paris, the first solo transatlantic flight, and became a hero around the world. (From the collection of Mishawaka-Penn Public Library.)

The women of this family gathered to socialize and have their picture made, just like the generation before them shown in the picture on the wall. (From the collection of Maureen Kronewitter Thomson.)

It was a cast of dozens—musicians, men, women, and children for the show at the Moose Hall, Mishawaka. (From the collection of Mishawaka-Penn Public Library.)

The Fraternal Order of Eagles began in Seattle in 1898. The organization originally consisted of theater actors, and as they toured they spread the membership throughout the United States and Canada. The brotherhood was the first fraternal order to offer members sick and funeral benefits. Frank Hering, a member of the South Bend Aerie, had been Notre Dame's first athletic director, a football quarterback, and baseball player. He revised the Eagles By-Laws and was known as the "Father of Mother's Day," having campaigned to set aside a special day for mothers. This photograph, taken in the 1930s, shows Eagles Lodge #283 in Mishawaka. (From the collection of Mishawaka-Penn Public Library.)

Music provided entertainment and some income for the LaCava family as they promoted Hoosier Beer. This photograph was taken in the 1940s in Mishawaka. (From the collection of Mishawaka-Penn Public Library.)

During World War II, women stepped into many men's roles, one of the most unusual being baseball. This 1945 photograph of the South Bend Blue Sox was taken at Bendix Field. Fourteen teams of women from Midwestern towns played professional baseball to crowds around the country from 1943 to 1954. (From the collection of Northern Indiana Historical Society Inc.-repository for the All-American Girls Professional Baseball League.)

In 1932, hundreds of kids showed up for the Buck Jones Club at the Tivoli in Mishawaka. Jones made more than 25 B Western movies from 1918 to 1942. (From the collection of Mishawaka-Penn Public Library.)

The theater was packed and the audience enthralled as the action packed Buck Jones western tore across the screen. (From the collection of Mishawaka-Penn Public Library.)

These gentlemen knew their birds, and the South Bend Homing Pigeon Club participated in the 1939 derby. Racing every weekend from April to October, the birds would find their way home from as much as 1,000-miles away. Five thousand area birds were retrained and donated

to the Army Signal Corp for the World War II effort. The private club also served as a tavern. (From the collection of Don Cornelis.)

With their bags packed, these women appear to be off to the world's fair on the Greyhound Bus. Round trip fares from Mishawaka to San Francisco AND New York were $69.95 in 1939 from the Peers News Depot and Bus Station at 121 North Main. (From the collection of Mishawaka-Penn Public Library.)

Five

THE PEOPLE

Dr. James F. Grimes (1825–1909.) came to
Mishawaka in 1853, and practiced medicine
for many years. (From the collection of
Hannah Lindahl Children's Museum.)

Most of the Wade sisters of New Carlisle married and raised families. One, however, attended St. Mary's College and became an artist. (From the collection of Pat Danielson Gloss.)

Fashion was important to the ladies of 1890. An outfit not only consisted of a long skirt and big-sleeved blouse, there were hats, ties, and shoes to consider. (From the collection of St. Joseph County Public Library.)

Henry Higgins, a Mishawaka jeweler, was commissioned to mint Civil War copper coins. Known as Primitive War tokens, they were necessary because people were hoarding gold and silver. In 1899 at the age of 16, his daughter Susie Higgins married Martin Beiger who owned the Ball Band, creating one of the richest families in the area. Susie died in 1927, leaving the Beiger Mansion for a women's home. The stately old home is now a privately owned B&B and restaurant. (From the collection of Hannah Lindahl Children's Museum.)

Marcus Webster (seated) came to the area in 1836 and farmed in Clay Township. He served in the Civil War and is shown with his family in 1900. (From the collection of Mary Zimmerman Waterson.)

The Powell family children were the first African Americans to graduate from Mishawaka High School. This school portrait was taken of Miss C.N. Powell in 1907. (From the collection of Hannah Lindahl Children's Museum.)

Grace Kroshaw and her sister had their picture made with their dolls in Three Oaks, Michigan, in the early part of the century. (From the collection of Hannah Lindahl Children's Museum.)

Harriet and Walter Witwer were raised in Mishawaka and lived in the area their entire lives. (From the collection of Harriet Witwer Marnon.)

The Kubiac family represents part of the strong Polish community that made the northern Indiana area their home in early-1900s. (From the collection of Helen Kubiac.)

Some photographs are timeless. This boy and his dog could be from almost any decade through the ages. (From the collection of St. Joseph County Public Library.)

A group of children can have fun anywhere, even sitting on a fence in the 1940s. (From the collection of Michelle Ottman Ashley.)

During the Depression Years, many families packed meager belongings in the car and headed west for greater opportunities. (From the collection of Maureen Kronewitter Thomson.)

Harriet Witwer rode the South Shore to the Chicago World's Fair in 1933 with a group of other Ball Band employees. She had this portrait cut there. (From the collection of Harriet Witwer Marnon.)

This girl had her picture taken with her pet bird, a bowl of eggs, and her doll and buggy. (From the collection of Mishawaka-Penn Public Library.)

Louella Thomson posed for this
photograph by the family car in 1931.
(From the collection of Maureen
Kronewitter Thomson.)

The Miltenberger family was part of
the German community of South Bend
in the 1920s. (From the collection of
Cheryl Lantz.)

After meeting on the train to the Chicago World's Fair in 1933, Harriet Witwer and Thomas Marnon were married and settled in Roseland to raise their family. (From the collection of Harriet Witwer Marnon.)

Photographs traced important life events. Here, Ed Wishin is pictured in 1930 with his First Communion class at St. Joseph in South Bend. (From the collection of Mary Heinerich Wishin.)

Merle, Joe, and Wade Danielson's parents had the boys' picture taken in New Carlisle, in 1914. All three went on to attend New Carlisle High School. (From the collection of Dennis Danielson.)

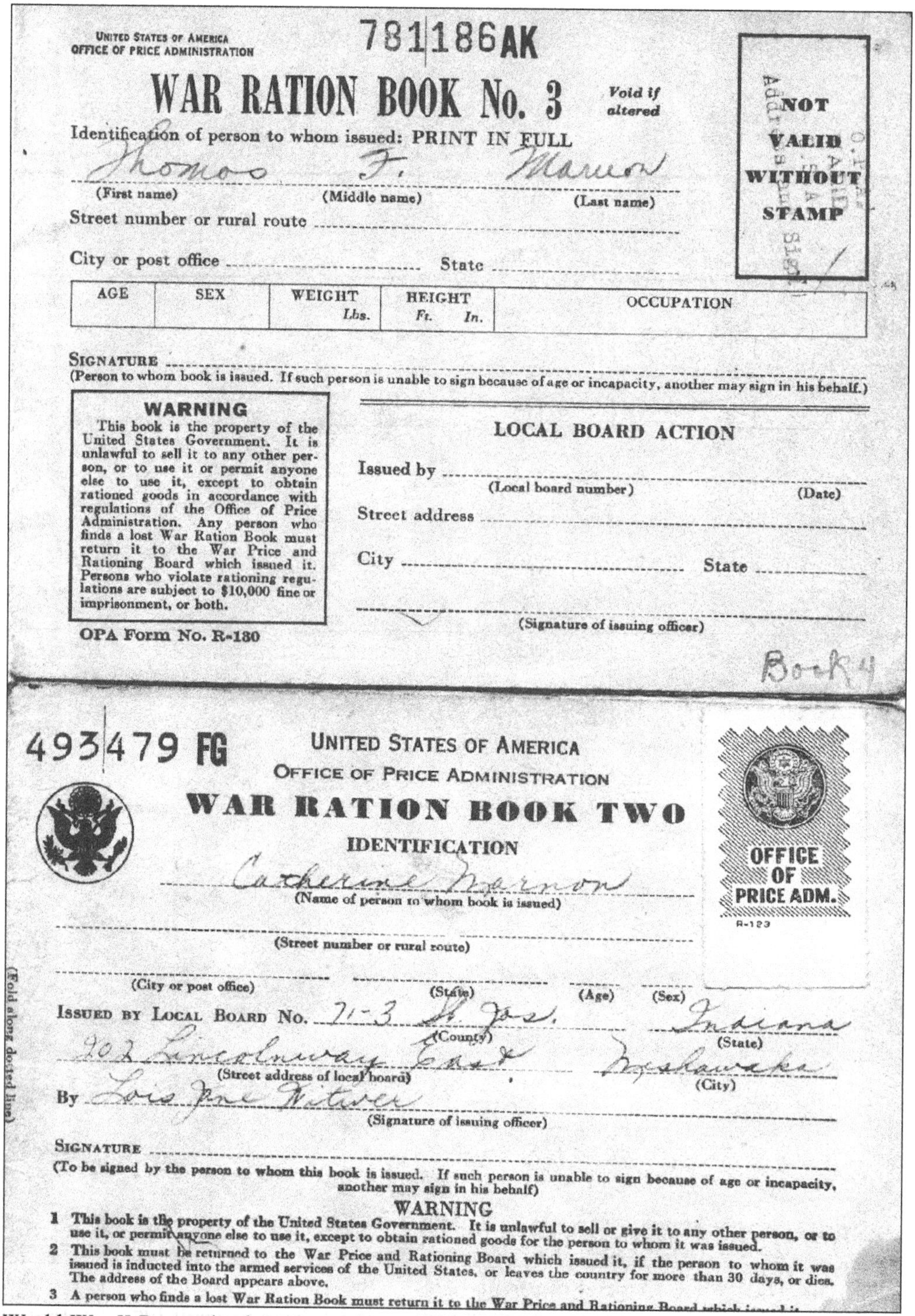

UNITED STATES OF AMERICA
OFFICE OF PRICE ADMINISTRATION

781186AK

WAR RATION BOOK No. 3

Void if altered

Identification of person to whom issued: PRINT IN FULL

Thomas   F.   Marmon

(First name)   (Middle name)   (Last name)

Street number or rural route ....

City or post office .... State ....

NOT VALID WITHOUT STAMP

AGE	SEX	WEIGHT Lbs.	HEIGHT Ft. In.	OCCUPATION

SIGNATURE ....
(Person to whom book is issued. If such person is unable to sign because of age or incapacity, another may sign in his behalf.)

WARNING
This book is the property of the United States Government. It is unlawful to sell it to any other person, or to use it or permit anyone else to use it, except to obtain rationed goods in accordance with regulations of the Office of Price Administration. Any person who finds a lost War Ration Book must return it to the War Price and Rationing Board which issued it. Persons who violate rationing regulations are subject to $10,000 fine or imprisonment, or both.

OPA Form No. R-130

LOCAL BOARD ACTION

Issued by ....
(Local board number)   (Date)

Street address ....

City .... State ....

(Signature of issuing officer)

Book 4

493479 FG

UNITED STATES OF AMERICA
OFFICE OF PRICE ADMINISTRATION

WAR RATION BOOK TWO

IDENTIFICATION

Catherine Marmon
(Name of person to whom book is issued)

....
(Street number or rural route)

....
(City or post office)   (State)   (Age)   (Sex)

ISSUED BY LOCAL BOARD NO. *71-3 St. Jos.*   *Indiana*
(County)   (State)

902 Lincolnway East   *Mishawaka*
(Street address of local board)   (City)

By *Lois June Witwer*
(Signature of issuing officer)

OFFICE OF PRICE ADM.
R-123

SIGNATURE ....
(To be signed by the person to whom this book is issued. If such person is unable to sign because of age or incapacity, another may sign in his behalf)

WARNING
1 This book is the property of the United States Government. It is unlawful to sell or give it to any other person, or to use it, or permit anyone else to use it, except to obtain rationed goods for the person to whom it was issued.
2 This book must be returned to the War Price and Rationing Board which issued it, if the person to whom it was issued is inducted into the armed services of the United States, or leaves the country for more than 30 days, or dies. The address of the Board appears above.
3 A person who finds a lost War Ration Book must return it to the War Price and Rationing Board which issued it.

World War II Ration books are seen here. "**WARNING** punishments ranging as high as Ten Years' Imprisonment or $10,000 Fine, or Both, may be imposed under United States Statues for violation of thereof arising out of infractions of Rationing Orders and Regulations. 'If you don't need it, DON'T BUY IT.'" (From the collection of Harriet Witwer Marnon.)

As a child in 1927, Mary Catherine Heinerich played games at her home in Roseland. As an adult, she joined the joined the Naval Security doing cryptanalysis to break German U-boat messages with the Engima coding machine during World War II. She received a Navy Intelligence Award for her work. (From the collection of Mary Heinerich Wishin.)

During the war years, a family member on leave was a time for celebration and family picnics with watermelons. Seen here is John Heinerich in South Bend in 1942. (From the collection of Mary Heinerich Wishin.)

117

Where there is industry there is scrap, and Berebitsky's Junk Yard on 400 West Indiana Avenue was a center of activity. Herman Ottman went to work in the yard at the age of 12 and stayed for 47 years as watchman and truck driver. He raised his family in the house adjoining the yard, and the children remember playing among the heaps of clothing and household goods. This photograph was taken in the 1950s in South Bend. (From the collection of Michelle Ottman Ashley.)

In 1948, these two girls often waited at the end of the road to welcome their father home from work. (From the collection of Maureen Kronewitter Thomson.)

Six

WHERE THEY LIVED

This log cabin is typical of the structures 1830s fur traders and settlers built for their families. (From the collection of St. Joseph County Public Library.)

Built in 1897, the Frederickson House is a fine example of Queen Ann Style, and is located at 233 North Lafayette in South Bend. (From the collection of Historic Preservation Commission of South Bend & St. Joseph County.)

The Frederickson House bathroom features ceramic tiled walls, a footed tub, and a copper hot water heater. (From the collection of Historic Preservation Commission of South Bend & St. Joseph County.)

The Frederickson House dining room includes a heavy oak table, a sideboard, and decorative leaded glass window, typical of the time. (From the collection of Historic Preservation Commission of South Bend & St. Joseph County.)

The Frederickson House music room illustrates the jam-packed decor of the time. (From the collection of Historic Preservation Commission of South Bend & St. Joseph County.)

Frank Lloyd Wright designed six houses in Indiana, two of which were in South Bend. This one built in 1906 is located at 715 West Washington, and a second built in 1948 is at 1404 Ridgedale Road. (From the collection of Historic Preservation Commission of South Bend & St. Joseph County.)

In 1880, the Clem and Cross families joined to have their picture taken at the Clem house in South Bend. (From the collection of Mary Zimmerman Waterson.)

American Four Square was built by the thousands between 1890 and 1940. This two-story square with a hipped roof had a one-story, full-width porch in front. A product of growth and technology, it was conceived as a result of rapidly growing cities. It was basically a box with eight nearly equal sized rooms and few protruding parts and could be assembled quickly. The Cornell model was available from Sears Roebuck in their 1908 catalog for $1,785. (From the collection of St. Joseph County Public Library.)

Built by David Moore in 1893, this house sat at 314 South Main in Mishawaka. (From the collection of Hannah Lindahl Children's Museum.)

123

By the turn of the century, South Bend had sufficient wealthy people to build and maintain a variety of fine houses. (From the collection of Dennis Danielson.)

Constructed for the Studebaker family in 1888 at an estimated cost of $250,000, Tippecanoe Place was a showcase at Washington and Taylor Streets in South Bend. The structure still serves the community, now as a fine restaurant and patrons are welcome to wander throughout the historic house. (From the collection of St. Joseph County Public Library.)

The Forest Avenue homes of 1894 were typical of the white-collar family residences. (From the collection of Historic Preservation Commission of South Bend & St. Joseph County.)

Overlooking the St. Joseph River and Leeper Park, the homes on Riverside Drive were built by some of South Bend's more affluent families. (From the collection of Historic Preservation Commission of South Bend & St. Joseph County.)

This farmhouse and barn are typical of a well-to-do family around the turn of the century. (From the collection of Historic Preservation Commission of South Bend & St. Joseph County.)

The Chapin House was built by one of South Bend's first merchants. The Gothic Revival house was constructed around 1855 and had five fireplaces and five baths. (From the collection of Historic Preservation Commission of South Bend & St. Joseph County.)

INDEX

CPSIA information can be obtained
at www.ICGtesting.com
Printed in the USA
LVHW102220041118
595946LV00014B/143/P